100 ANY-SIZE FLOWER BLOCKS
by Rita Weiss & Linda Causee

Before You Start

Choose the block you want to make. Inside this book, you will find a self-loading CD that contains 100 Flower quilt block patterns in several sizes. There are blocks that use foundation piecing, traditional appliqué, picture appliqué or patchwork templates. The files on the CD are easily opened using Adobe® Reader®. If you don't have Adobe® Reader® on your computer you can get a free download at http://www.adobe.com/. The site provides easy, step-by-step instructions for the download.

When you are ready to make your quilt, simply print out the required pattern(s) for your block(s). If you choose a foundation-pieced or picture appliqué block, print out the pattern in the size you desire: 4", 5", 6", 7" or 8". If you would like to make a 10" block, you will need to visit your local copy store and enlarge a 5" block by 200% then print it out on 11" x 17" paper. If you choose a traditional appliqué or patchwork block (4", 6", 8", 10", 12" or 16", with a few being 5", 7½", 10", 12½", or 15"), print out the templates needed for your block, then glue the templates on to plastic or heavy cardboard. When you are certain that your glue has dried, cut out your templates. If your templates become worn, simply repeat the process.

LEISURE ARTS, INC.
Maumelle, Arkansas

PRODUCED BY

PRODUCTION TEAM

Creative Directors:	Jean Leinhauser and Rita Weiss
Book Design:	Linda Causee
Technical Editor:	Ann Harnden
Block Diagrams:	April McArthur

We have made every effort to ensure that these instructions are accurate and complete. We cannot, however, be responsible for human error, typographical mistakes or variations in individual work.

PUBLISHED BY LEISURE ARTS, INC.

© 2014 by Leisure Arts, Inc.

104 Champs Boulevard, STE. 100

Maumelle, AR 72113

www. leisurearts.com

Library of Congress Control Number: 2014940359

ISBN: 978-1-4647-1591-4

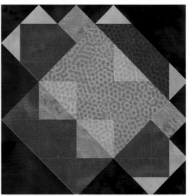

Introduction

If you love flowers, as we do, then you probably enjoy their beauty in your garden or with lovely bouquets in the rooms of your house. But, what do you do when the weather no longer supports flower gardens? How do you continue your love of flowers then?

If you are like us, we can't imagine not using flower designs in our quilts. So, we've collected 100 flower patterns for you to use. Look through the pages of quilt blocks and choose your favorites. You can create an entire quilt by repeating one block, or elect to make a sampler quilt or wall hanging with many different blocks. If making a full-size bed quilt is too large a task at this time, why not make a wall hanging or even a floral placemat like the ones we show on page 62.

In this book, you'll find that there are four different kinds of blocks: blocks that use patchwork templates, blocks that use foundation piecing and blocks that use traditional appliqué or picture appliqué. Whether you are an experienced quilt maker or just a beginner, you may agree that one of the most difficult parts of a project is finding the necessary patterns or templates, no matter which technique you choose.

Find the answer to that problem in this book and its enclosed CD! For applique and foundation piecing designs, just place the CD into your computer, click on the block of your choice in the size that you want and print out the patterns you'll need. For traditional patchwork designs, print out the templates you need for one of the available block sizes and glue them onto plastic or heavy cardboard. If your original templates become worn, or if you need additional pieces, just repeat the process.

If you've forgotten—or if you've never learned how to make a quilt, we've included some basic instructions on the CD.

So get ready to add a colorful addition to your home. Make a miniature quilt, a wall hanging, a twin size bed quilt, or even a king size quilt. Then be prepared to receive applause from every flower lover who lives in your home or just stops by for a visit.

Contents

Cosmos
Foundation Piecing

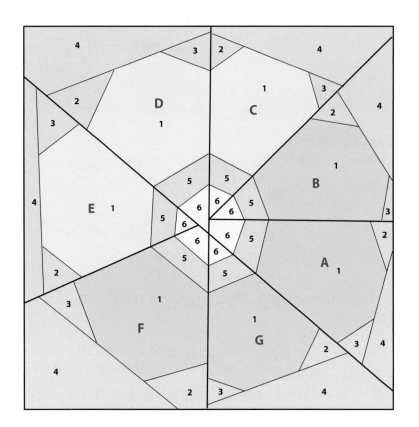

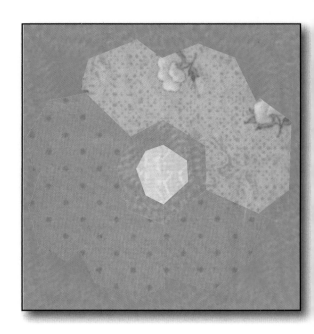

Tiger Lily
Foundation Piecing

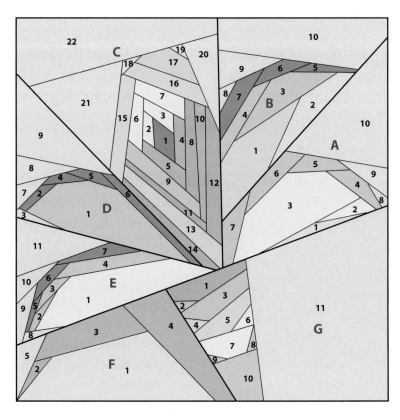

Daisy
Foundation Piecing

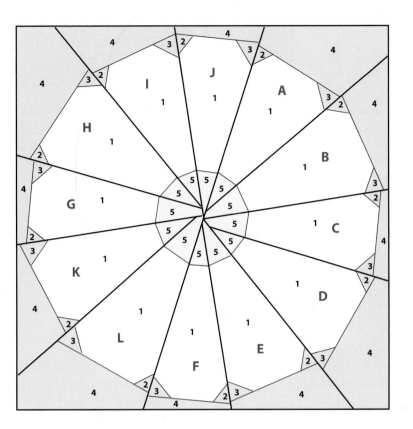

Bird of Paradise
Foundation Piecing

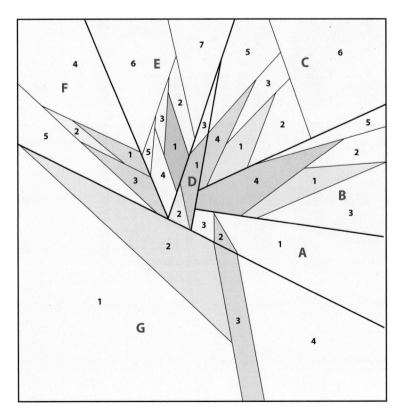

Daffodil

Foundation Piecing

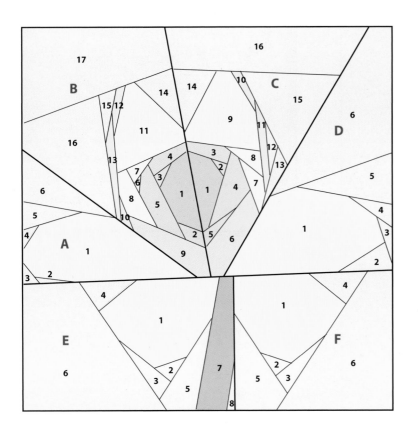

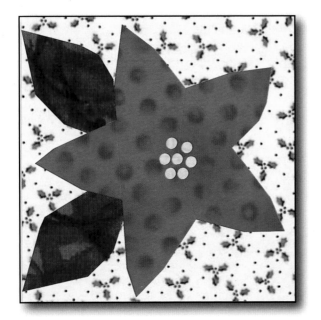

Poinsettia

Foundation Piecing

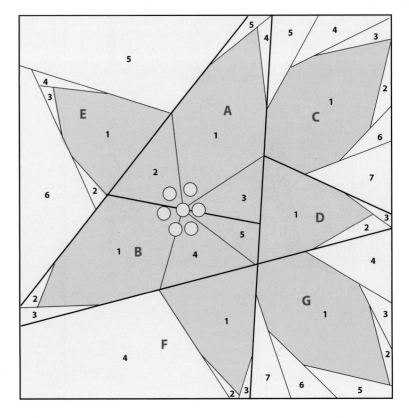

Tulip

Foundation Piecing

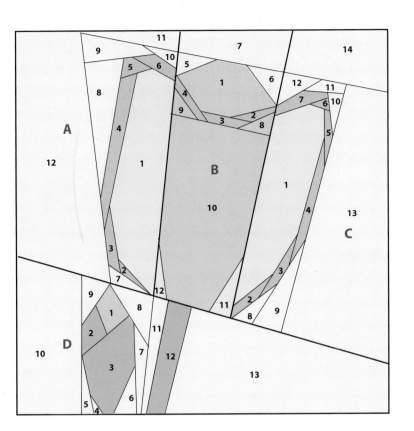

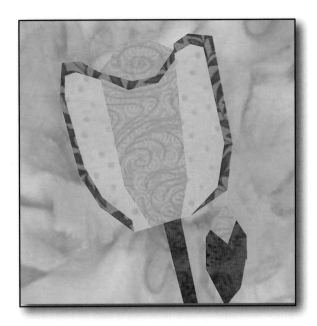

Pansy

Foundation Piecing

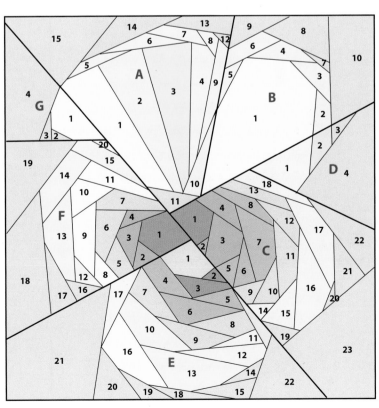

Sunflower
Foundation Piecing

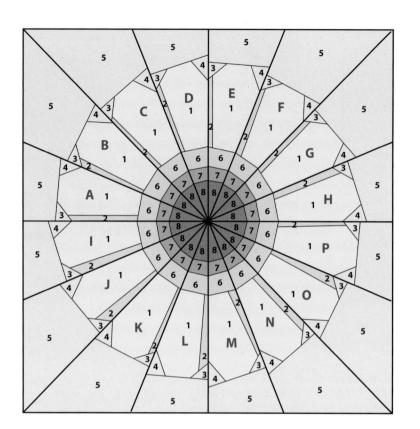

Calla Lily
Foundation Piecing

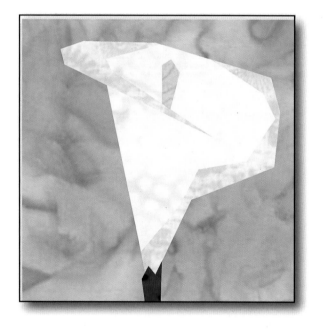

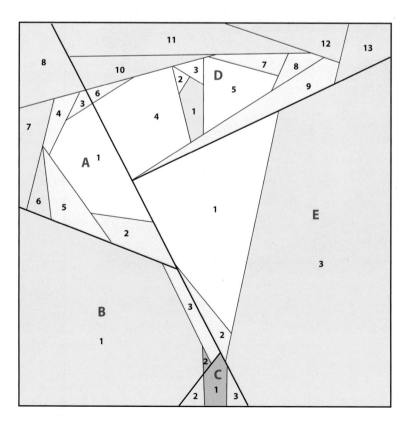

8

Violet

Foundation Piecing

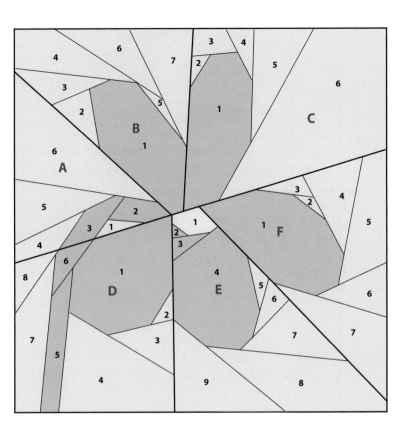

Potted Tulip

Foundation Piecing

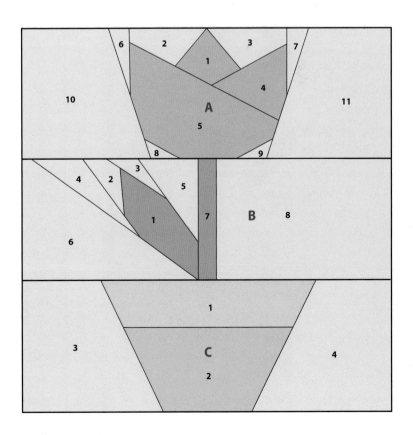

Potted Flower

Foundation Piecing

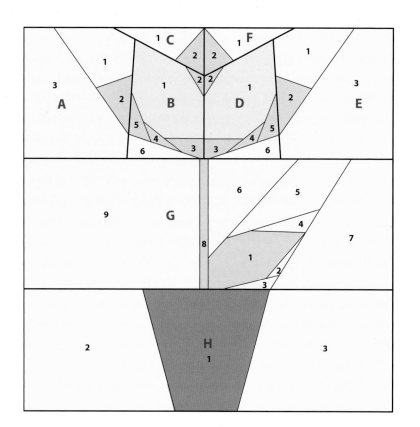

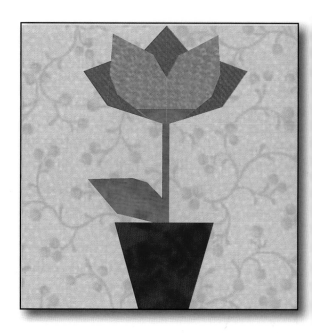

Potted Posy

Foundation Piecing

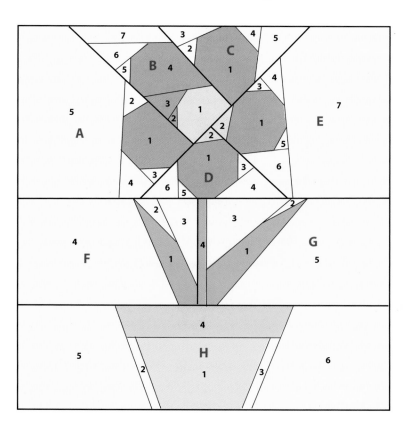

10

Star Flower
Foundation Piecing

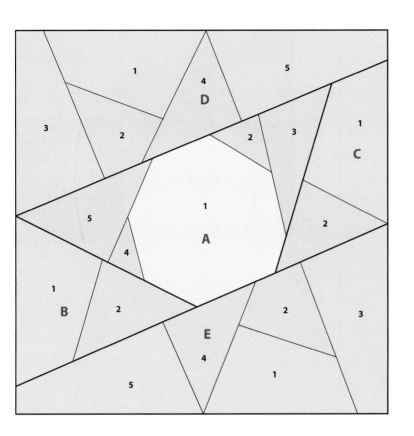

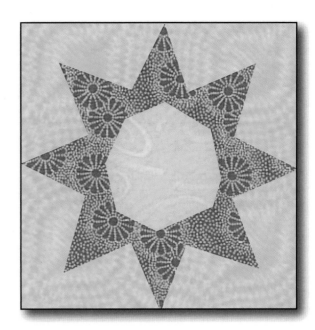

Single Tulip
Foundation Piecing

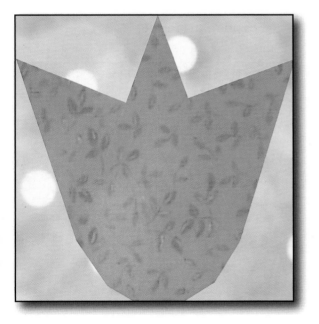

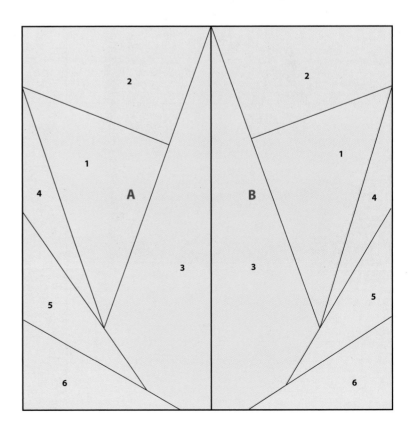

Tulip Star
Foundation Piecing

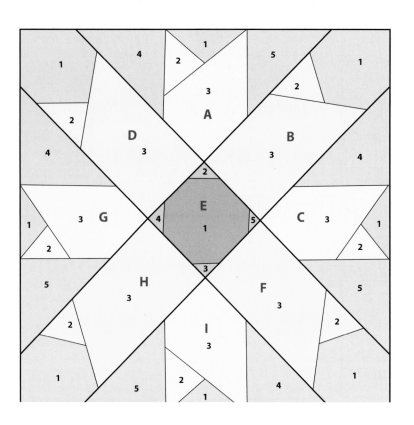

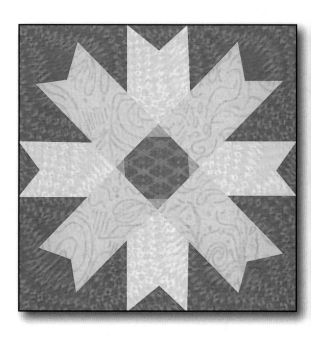

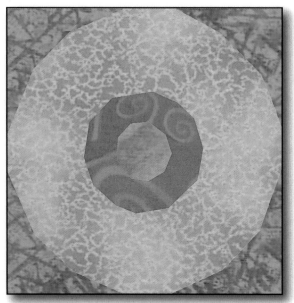

Circle Flower
Foundation Piecing

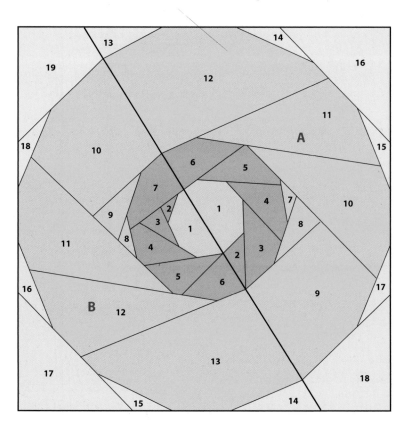

Aster

Foundation Piecing

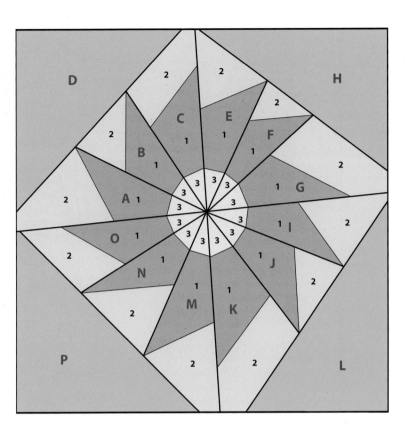

Marigold Pair

Foundation Piecing

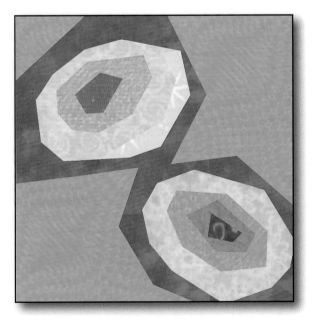

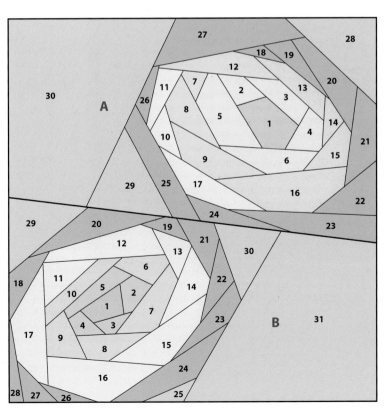

Log Cabin Flower

Foundation Piecing

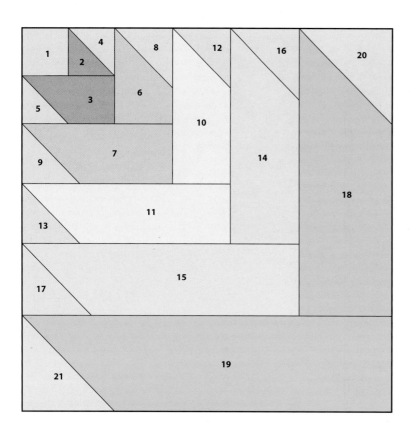

Log Cabin Bud

Foundation Piecing

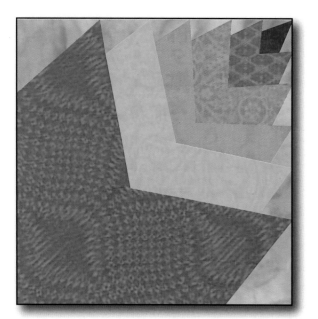

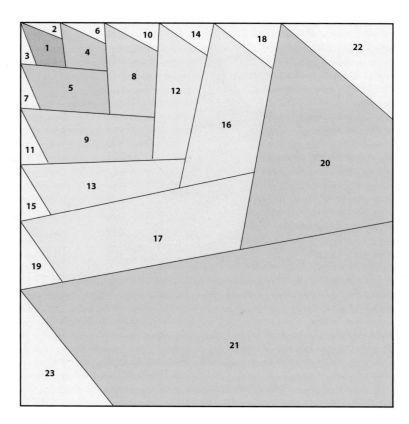

Crazy Rose
Foundation Piecing

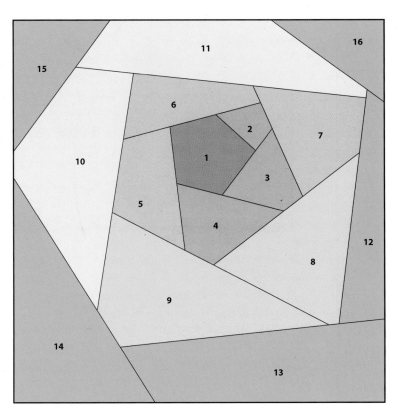

Log Cabin Squash Flower
Foundation Piecing

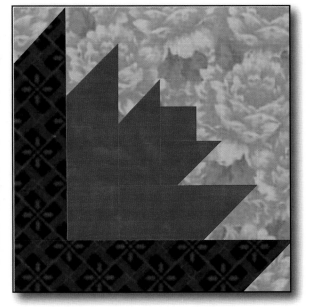

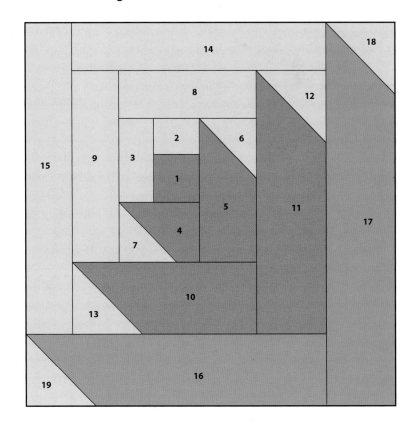

Log Cabin Flower Bud
Foundation Piecing

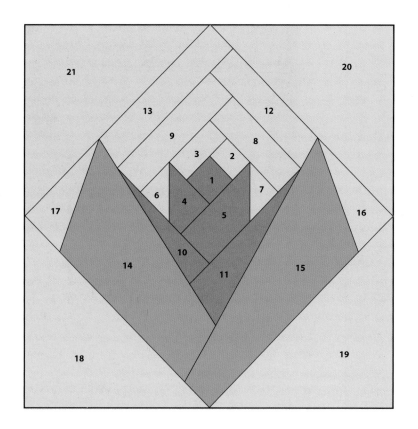

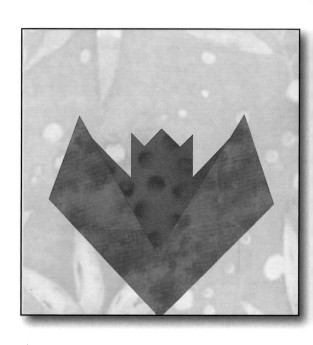

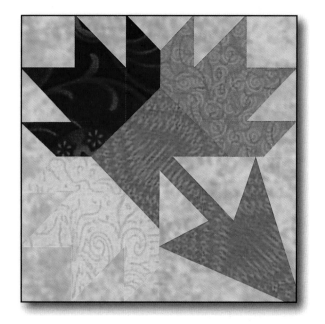

Lily Bouquet
Foundation Piecing

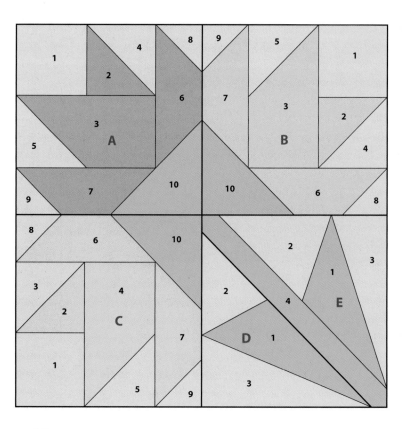

Log Cabin Lily

Foundation Piecing

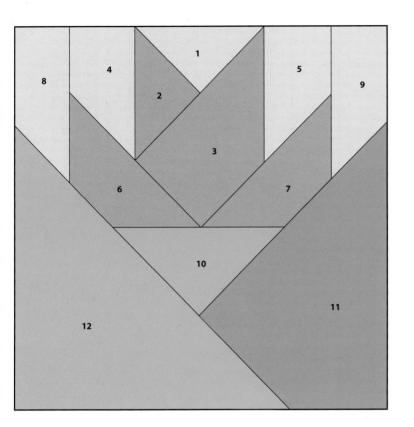

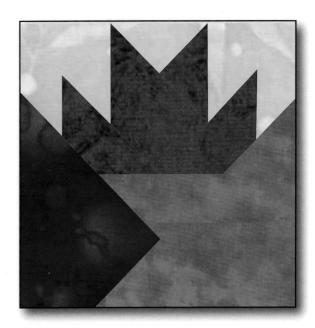

Log Cabin Crocus

Foundation Piecing

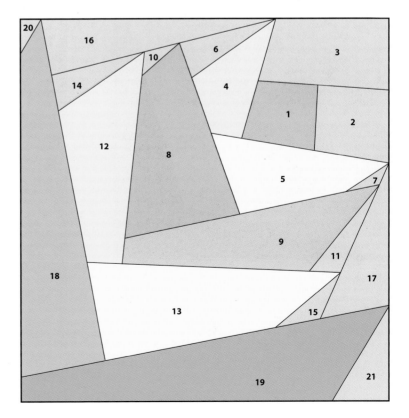

Log Cabin Crazy Flower

Foundation Piecing

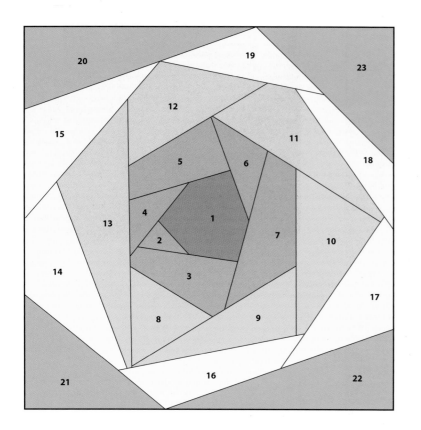

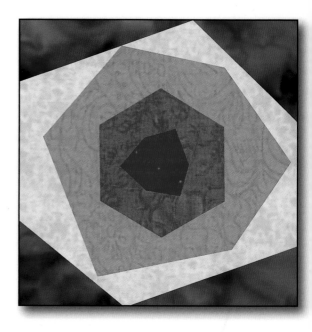

Log Cabin Crazy Bud

Foundation Piecing

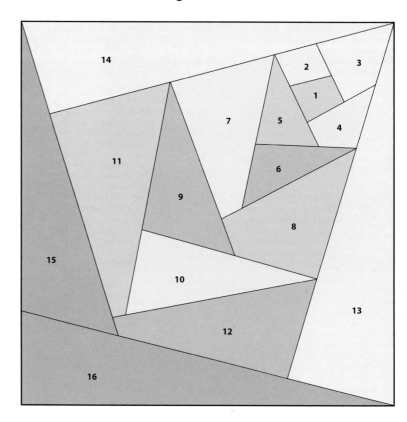

Pointy Flower

Foundation Piecing

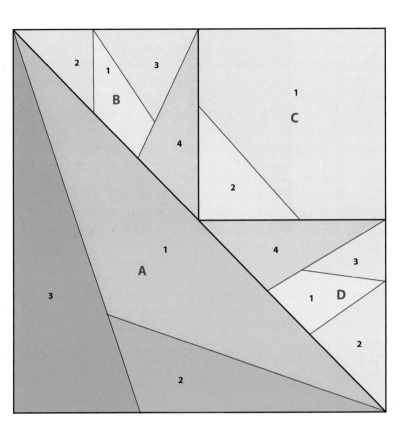

Flower Basket

Foundation Piecing

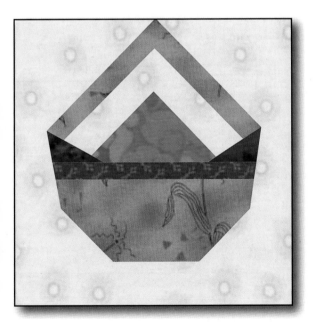

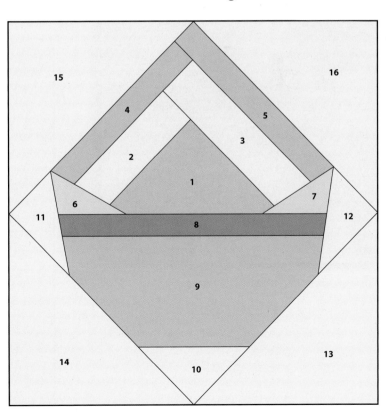

Simple Bud
Foundation Piecing

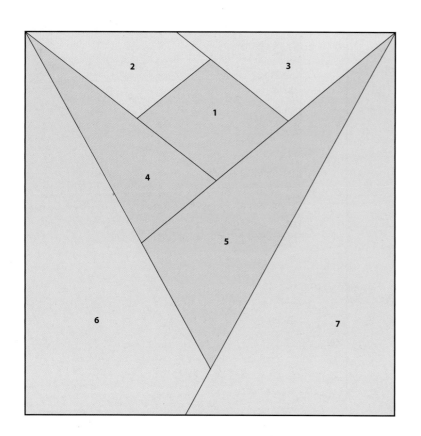

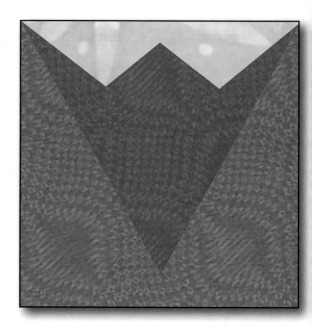

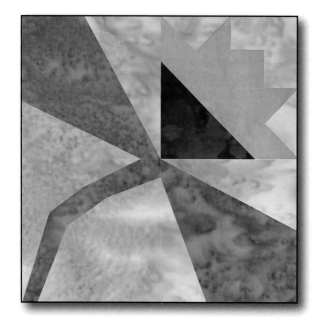

Blooming Flower
Foundation Piecing

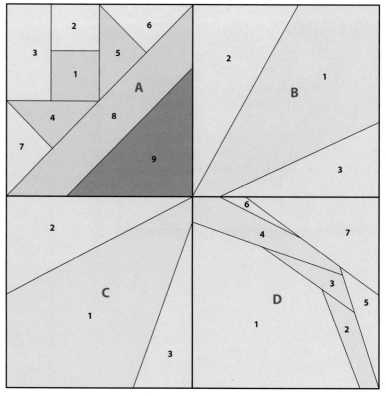

Triangle Tulip

Foundation Piecing

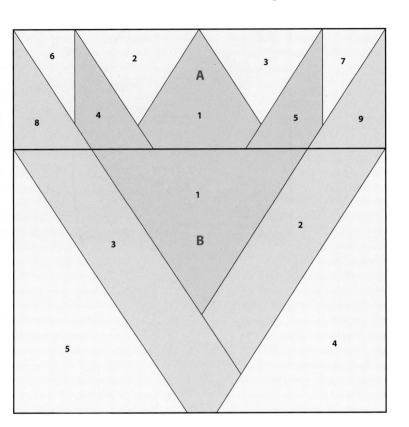

Diagonal Flower Basket

Foundation Piecing

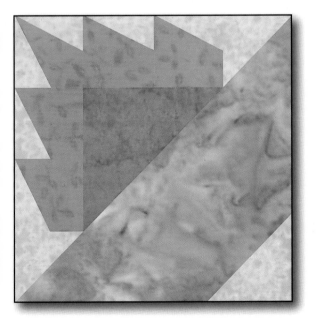

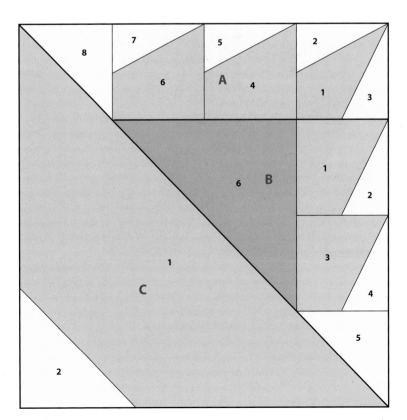

21

Nosegay Bud

Foundation Piecing

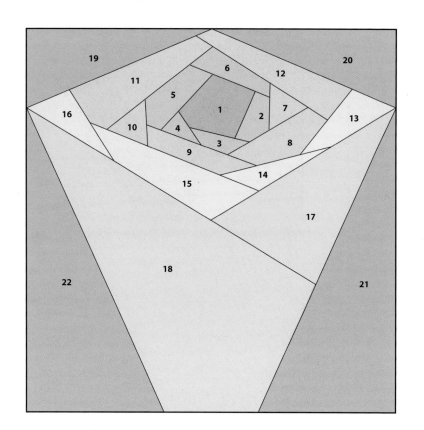

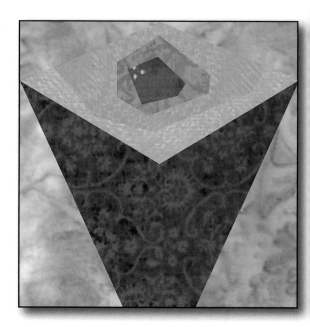

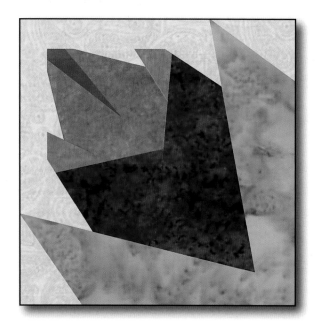

Budding Rose

Foundation Piecing

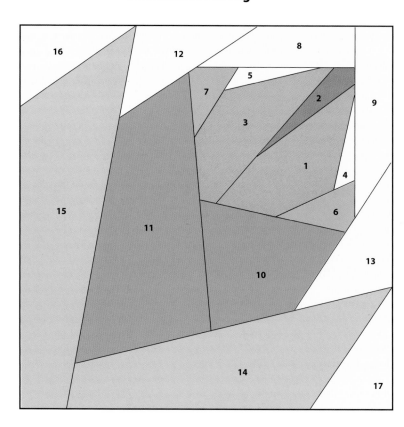

Corner Tulips

Foundation Piecing

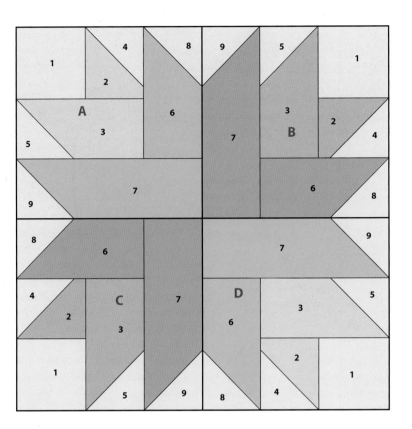

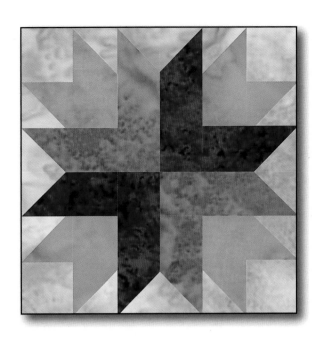

Diamond Flowers

Foundation Piecing

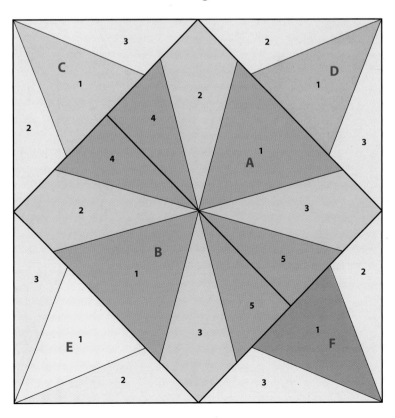

23

Posy Flower Pot

Picture Appliqué

Pretty Flower

Picture Appliqué

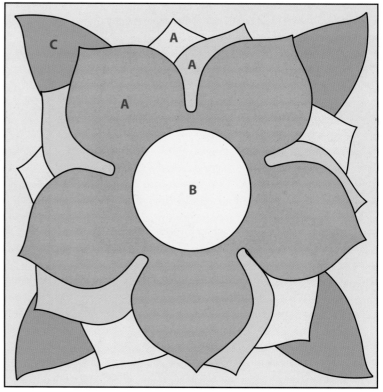

5-Petal Flower
Picture Appliqué

Regal Rose
Picture Appliqué

Simple Tulip

Picture Appliqué

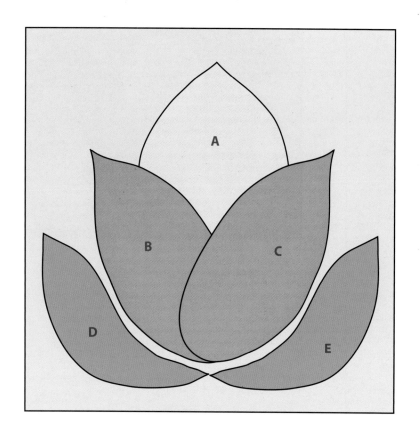

Water Lily

Picture Appliqué

26

Petite Flowers

Picture Appliqué

Ragged Flower

Picture Appliqué

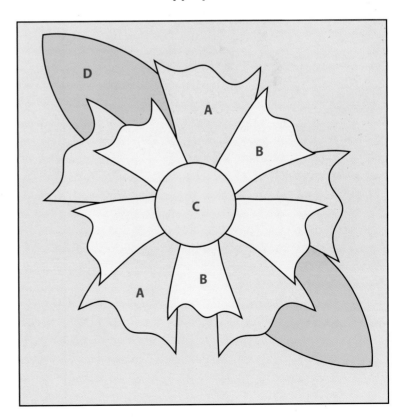

Rose Bud

Picture Appliqué

Sweet Pea

Picture Appliqué

Begonias in a Wreath

Traditional Appliqué

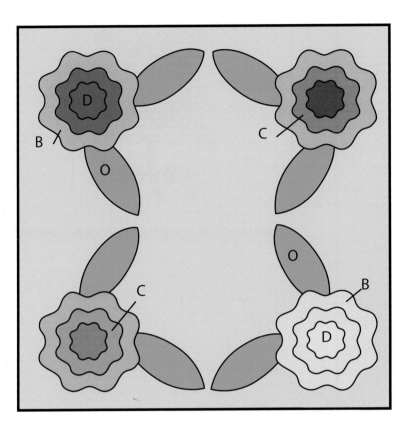

Hibiscus

Traditional Appliqué

Peony

Traditional Appliqué

Petunias in a Wreath

Traditional Appliqué

Rose of Sharon

Traditional Appliqué

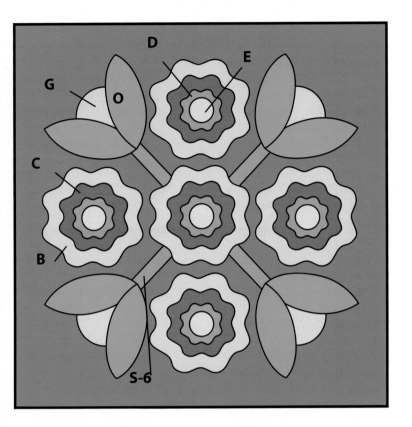

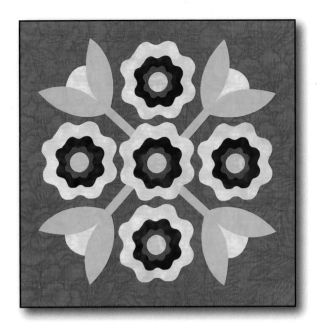

Victorian Rose

Traditional Appliqué

Washington Rose

Traditional Appliqué

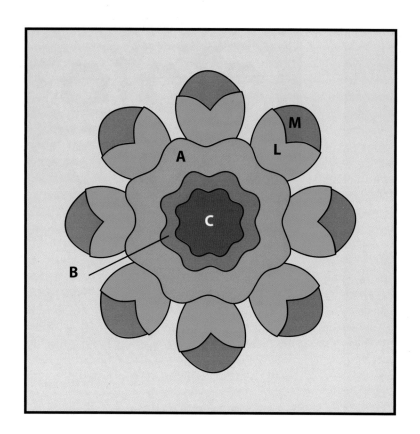

Whig Rose

Traditional Appliqué

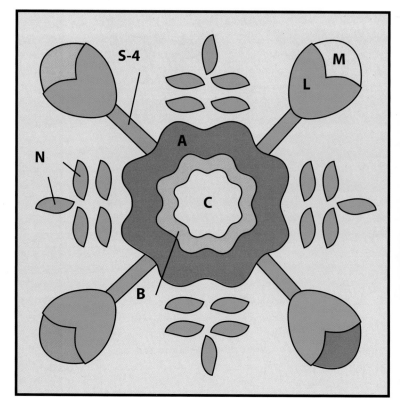

Wild Rose

Traditional Appliqué

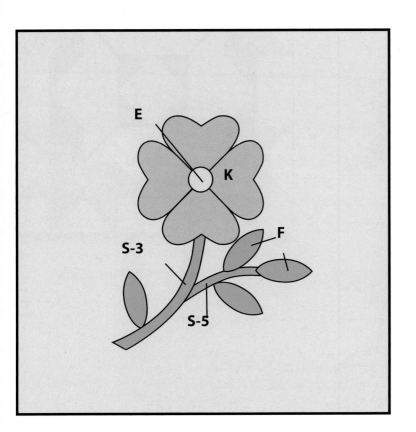

Wreath of Flowers

Traditional Appliqué

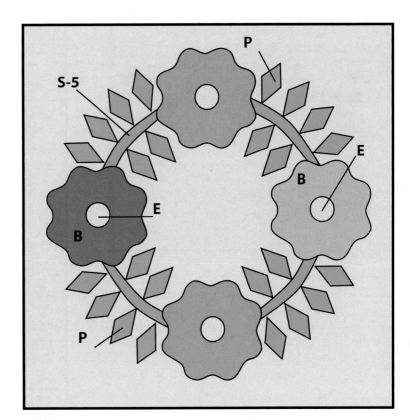

Double Tulip

Patchwork - Four-Patch

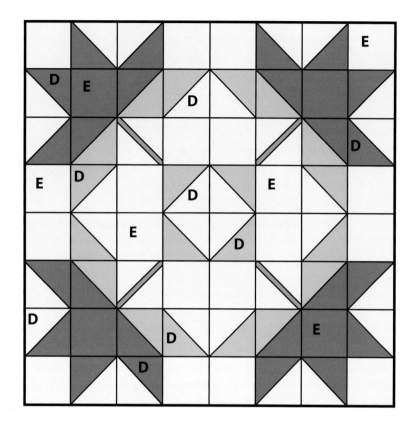

Note: *Embroider or appliqué stems after piecing block.*

Chrysanthemum

Patchwork - Four-Patch

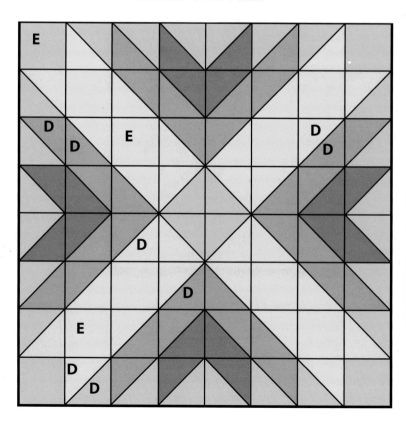

Cleveland Tulip

Patchwork - Four-Patch

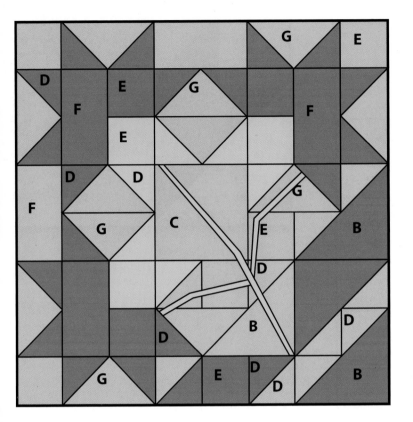

Note: *Embroider or appliqué stems after piecing block.*

Crocus

Patchwork - Four-Patch

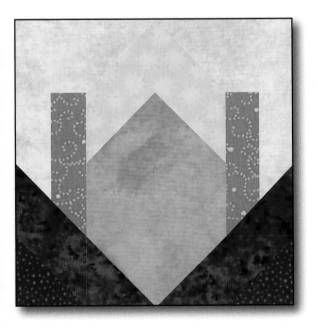

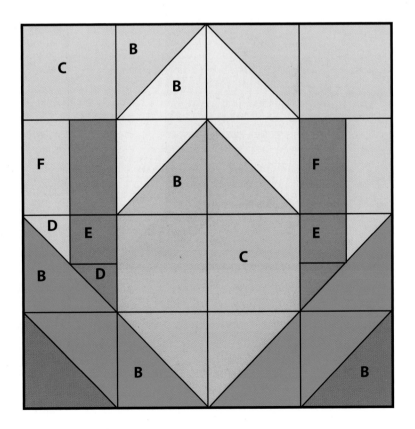

Patchwork Flower Basket

Patchwork - Four-Patch

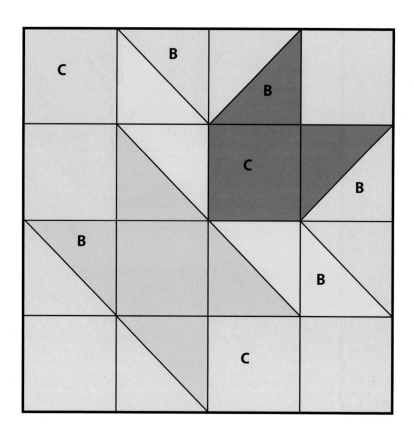

Colorful Crocus

Patchwork - Five-Patch

Diamond Rose
Patchwork - Four-Patch

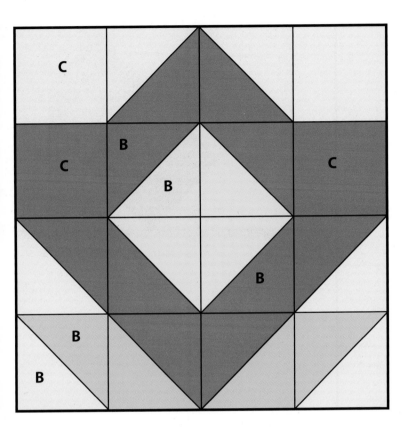

Dutch Rose
Patchwork - Four-Patch

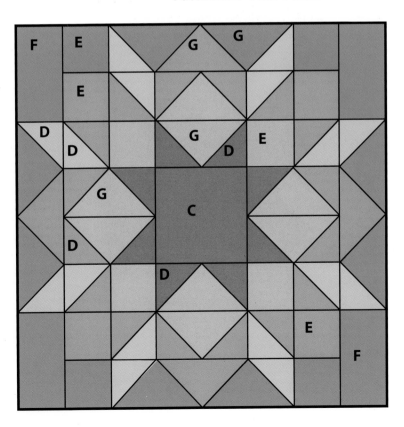

Iris Rainbow
Patchwork - Four-Patch

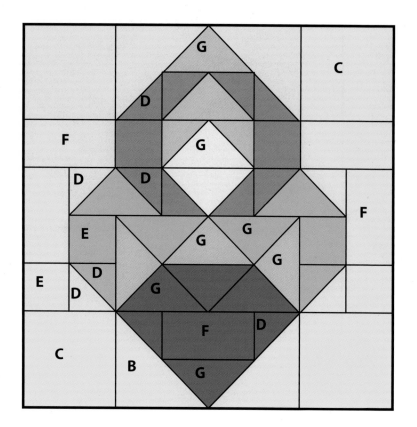

Iris
Patchwork - Four-Patch

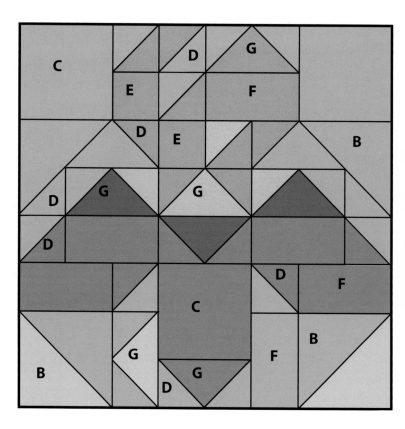

Jack-in-the-Pulpit

Patchwork - Five-Patch

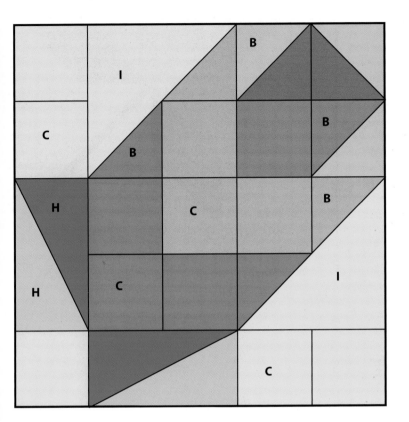

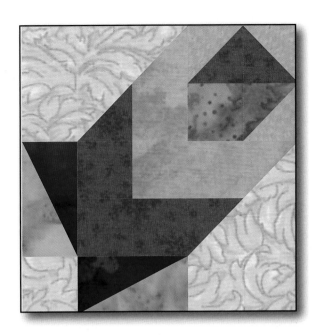

Note: *Embroider or appliqué stems after piecing block.*

Royal Dutch Tulip

Patchwork - Four-Patch

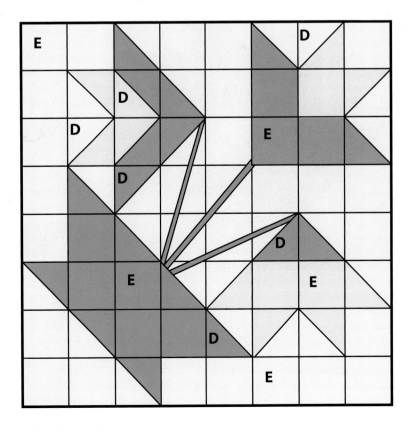

Single Lily

Patchwork - Four-Patch

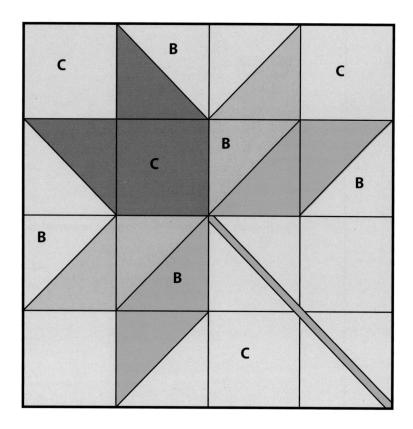

Note: *Embroider or appliqué stems after piecing block.*

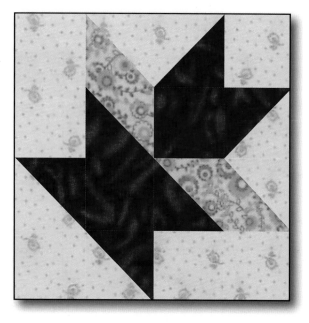

Jersey Tulip

Patchwork - Four-Patch

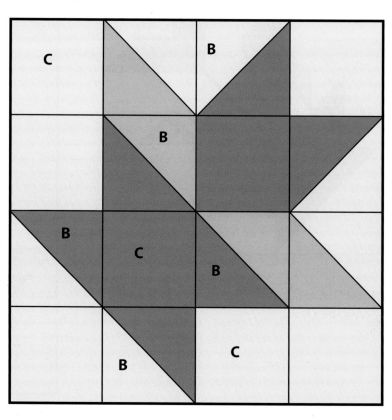

Lilies

Patchwork - Four-Patch

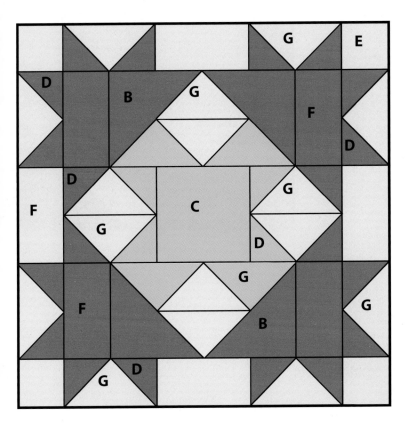

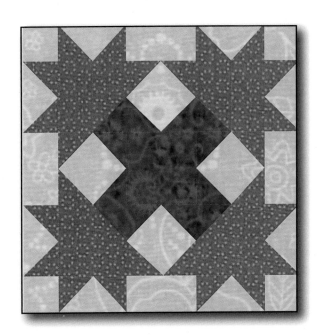

Note: *Embroider or appliqué stems after piecing block.*

Potted Lilies

Patchwork - Four-Patch

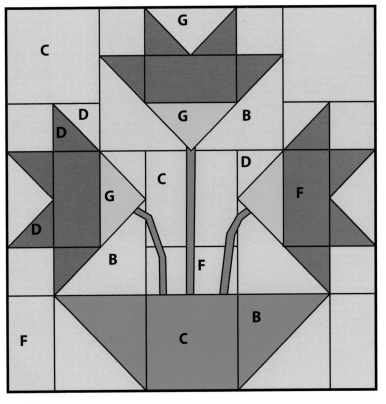

41

Lotus
Patchwork - Five-Patch

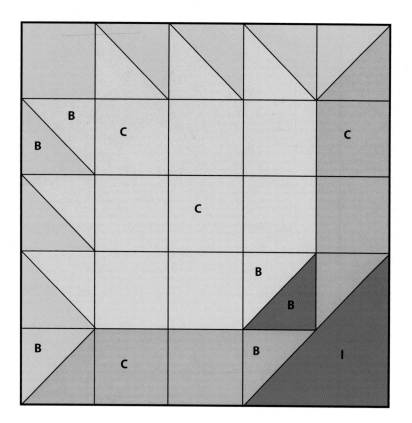

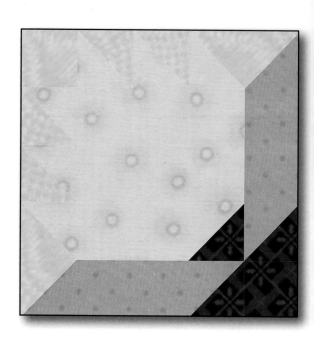

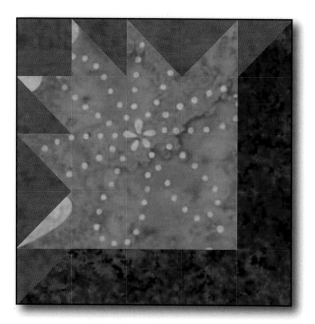

Magnolia
Patchwork - Five-Patch

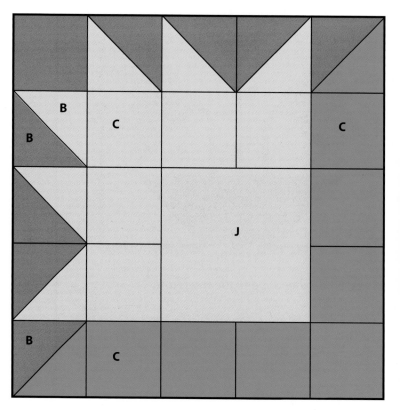

White Magnolia

Patchwork - Five-Patch

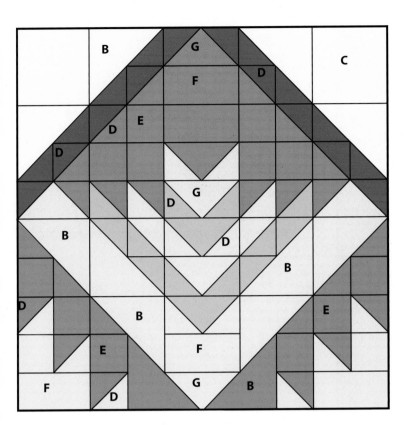

Marigold Garden

Patchwork - Five-Patch

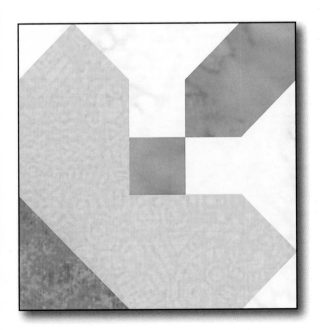

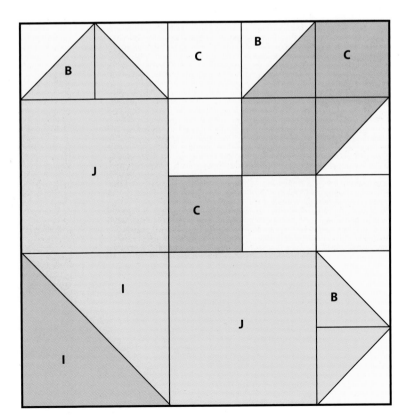

Nosegay
Patchwork - Five-Patch

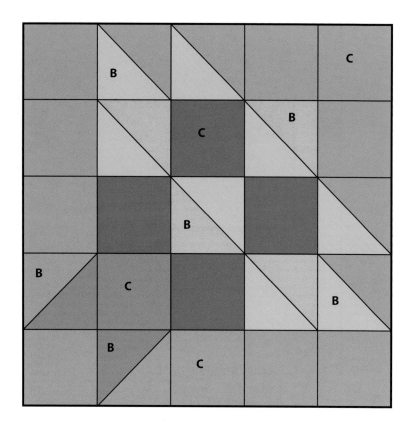

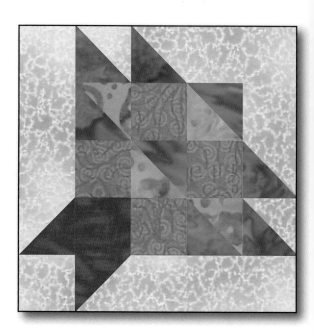

Oriental Rose
Patchwork - Five-Patch

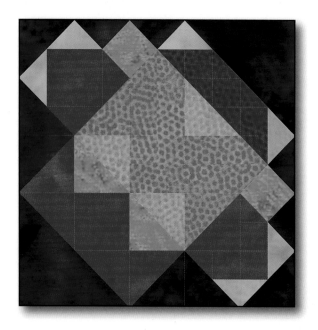

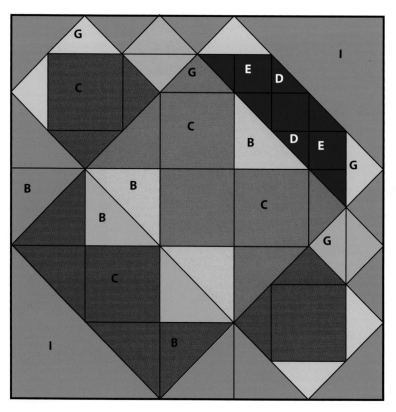

Peonies

Patchwork - Four-Patch

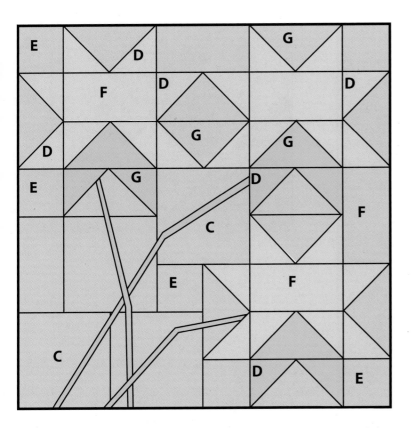

Note: *Embroider or appliqué stems after piecing block.*

Poinsettia Blossom

Patchwork - Four-Patch

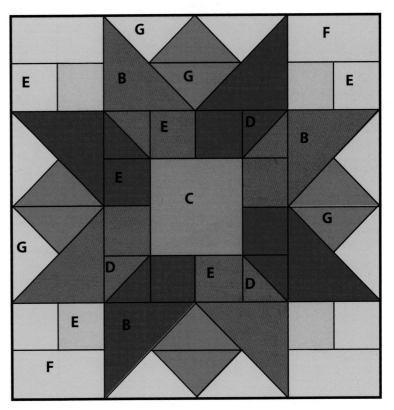

Poinsettia
Patchwork - Four-Patch

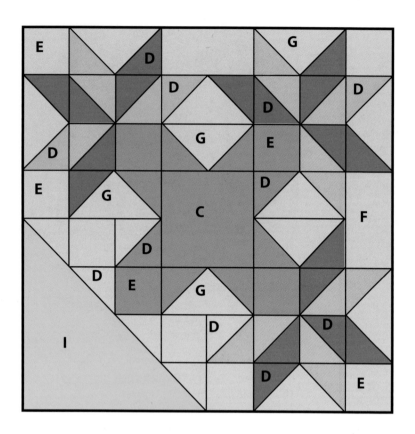

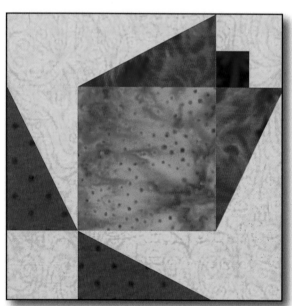

Rose Trellis
Patchwork - Four-Patch

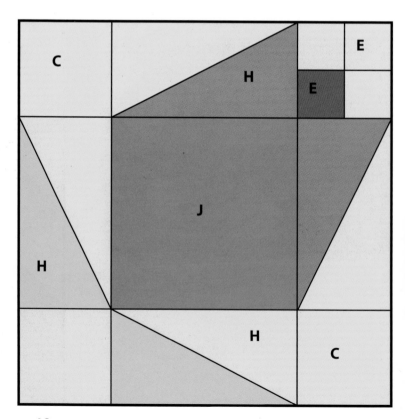

Patchwork Rosebud

Patchwork - Five-Patch

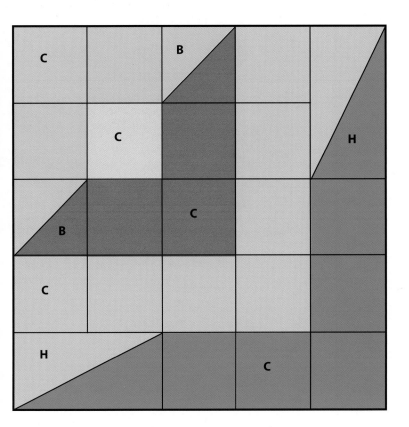

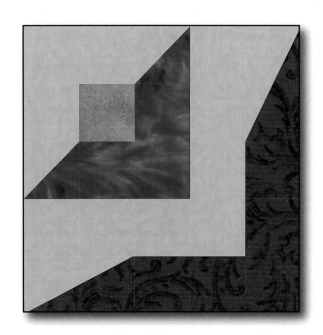

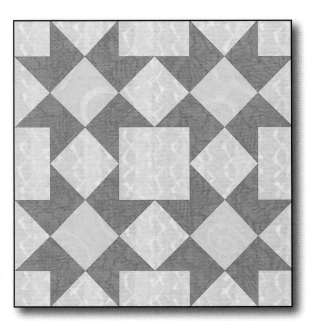

Sunflowers

Patchwork - Four-Patch

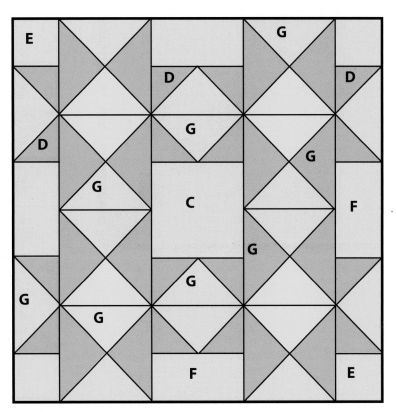

Texas Bluebonnet

Patchwork - Four-Patch

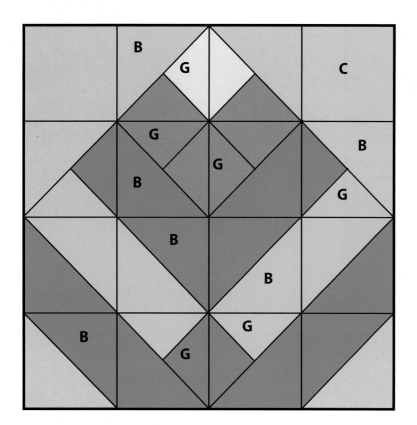

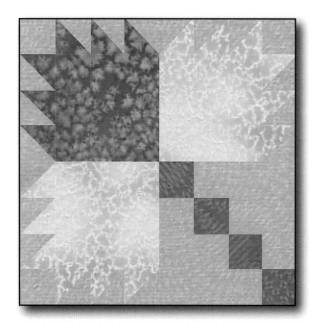

Thistle

Patchwork - Four-Patch

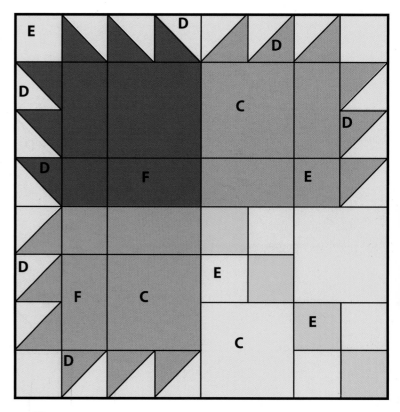

48

Trumpet Flower

Patchwork - Four-Patch

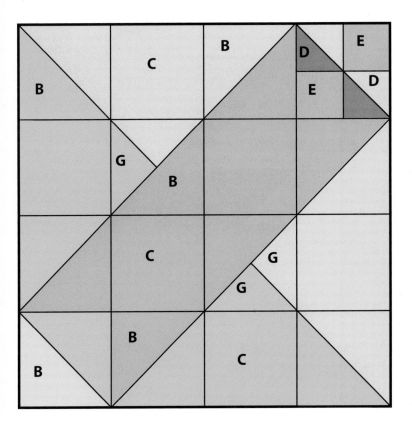

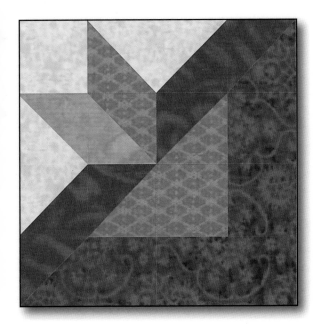

Patchwork Tulip

Patchwork - Four-Patch

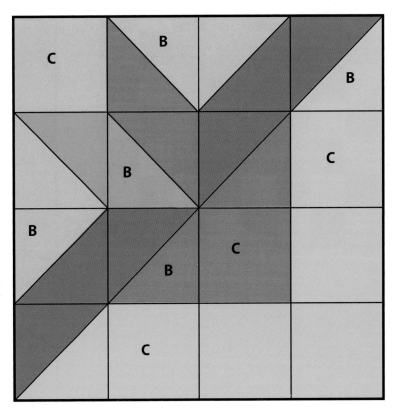

Tulip on an Angle

Patchwork - Five-Patch

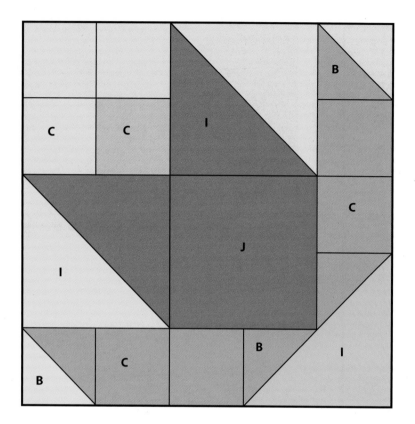

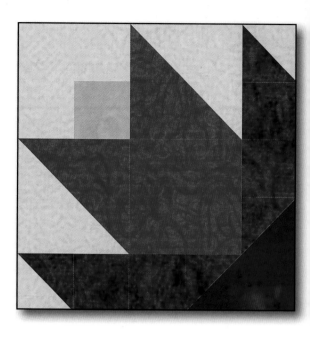

Tulip Tile

Patchwork - Four-Patch

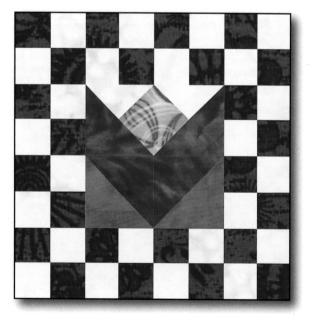

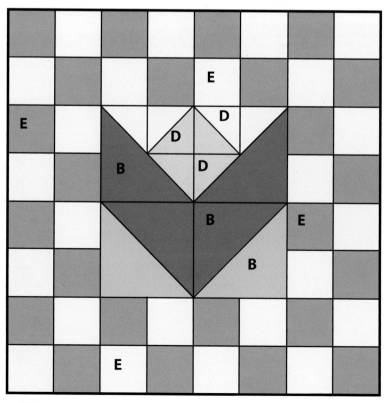

Skinny Tulip

Patchwork - Five-Patch

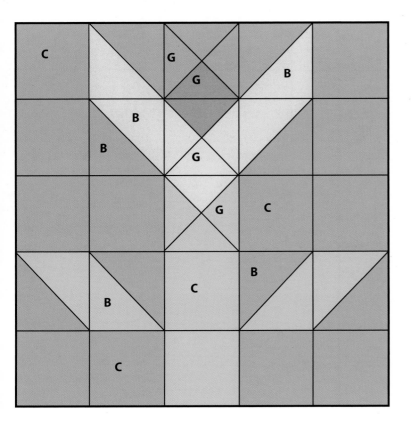

Note: *Embroider or appliqué stems after piecing block.*

White Lily

Patchwork - Four-Patch

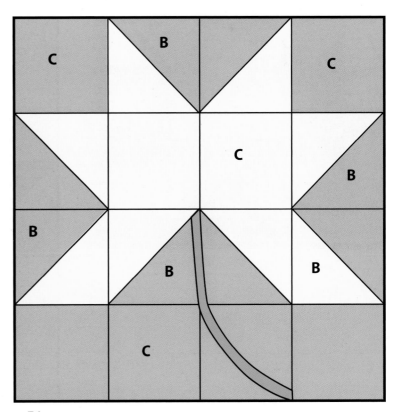

Windblown Lily

Patchwork - Four-Patch

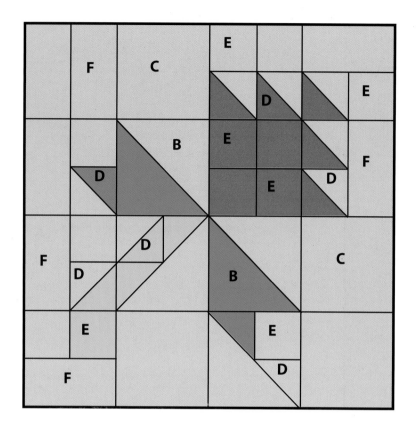

Winter Rose Poinsettia

Patchwork - Four-Patch

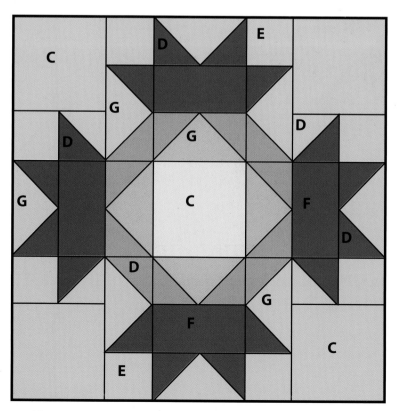

Zygocactus
Patchwork - Five-Patch

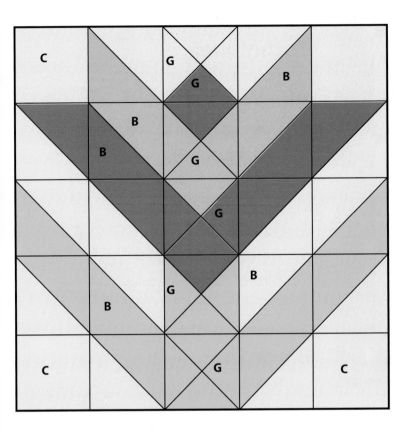

Climbing Roses
Patchwork - Five-Patch

Flower Garden

Foundation Piecing

Approximate Size:
36 ½" x 36 ½"

Technique:
Foundation Piecing

Blocks:
Cosmos (page 4)

Violet (page 9)

Calla Lily (page 8)

Pansy (page 7)

Tulip (page 7)

Daffodil (page 6)

Bird of Paradise (page 5)

Daisy (page 5)

Tiger Lily (page 4)

Block Size:
8" x 8"

MATERIALS:
1 yard light green

¼ yard red

¼ yard burgundy

fat quarter dark yellow

½ yard med green

¼ yard med-dark green

¼ yard dark geen

¾ yard backing

Batting

CUTTING:
Blocks

Note: *You don't need to cut exact pieces for foundation piecing.*

Finishing

24 strips, 2 ½" x 8 ½", dark green (sashing)

16 squares, 2 ½" x 2 ½", light green (cornerstones)

4 strips, 3 ½"-wide, medium-dark green (border)

4 strips, 2 ½"-wide, dark green (binding)

INSTRUCTIONS:
1. Make nine foundation-pieced flower blocks referring to Foundation Piecing on the enclosed CD.

2. Referring to photo, sew blocks in three rows of three blocks. Sew alternating rows of sashing and cornerstones.

3. Sew the rows of blocks and sashing together.

4. Sew border to quilt top sides first, then top and bottom.

5. Finish quilt referring to Finishing your Quilt on the CD.

Window Garden

Foundation Piecing

Approximate Size:
39 ½" x 20 ½"

Technique:
Foundation Piecing

Blocks:
Potted Posy (page 10)
Potted Tulip (page 9)
Potted Flower (page 10)

Block Size:
8" x 8"

MATERIALS:
½ yard light blue
¼ yard medium pink
⅛ yard brown
¾ yard medium green
¼ yard dark green
scraps purple, yellow, red, light pink, light green, orange
¾ yard backing
Batting

CUTTING:
Blocks
Note: *You don't need to cut exact pieces for foundation piecing.*

Finishing
4 strips, 2" x 8 ½", light blue (sashing)
1 strip, 2" x 30 ½", light blue (top sashing)
1 strip, 2" x 30 ½", brown (bottom sashing)
3 strips, 2"-wide, medium pink (first border)
3 strips, 3 ½" -wide, medium green (second border)
3 strips, 2 ½"-wide, dark green (binding)

INSTRUCTIONS:
1. Make 3 foundation-pieced flower blocks referring to Foundation Piecing on the CD.

2. Referring to photo, sew blocks together with 2" x 8 ½" light blue strips in between.

3. Sew 2" x 30 ½" light blue strip to top of block row; sew 2" x 30 ½" brown strip to bottom of block row.

4. Sew the 2"-wide medium pink strips to sides of quilt first, then to top and bottom.

5. Sew green 3 ½"-wide border strips to quilt top sides first, then to top and bottom.

6. Finish quilt referring to Finishing your Quilt on the CD.

Flower Log Cabin
Foundation Piecing

Approximate Size:
60 ½" x 76"
Technique:
Foundation Piecing
Blocks:
Log Cabin Flower
(page 14)
Block Size:
8" x 8"

MATERIALS:
2 ½ yards light blue
2 yards red
2 yards green
¾ yard backing
Batting

CUTTING:
Blocks
Note: *You don't need to cut exact pieces for foundation piecing.*

Finishing
8 strips, 2 ½" - wide, red (first border)
8 strips, 4 ½" - wide, green (second border)
8 strips, 2 ½" - wide, green (binding)

INSTRUCTIONS:
1. Referring to Foundation Piecing on the CD, make 48 Log Cabin Flower blocks.

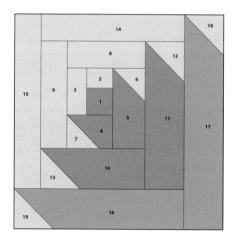

2. Referring to photo, arrange blocks in eight rows of six blocks. Sew together in rows, then sew rows together.

3. Sew first and second borders to quilt top sides first, then top and bottom.

4. Finish quilt referring to Finishing your Quilt on the CD.

Flower Path
Foundation Piecing

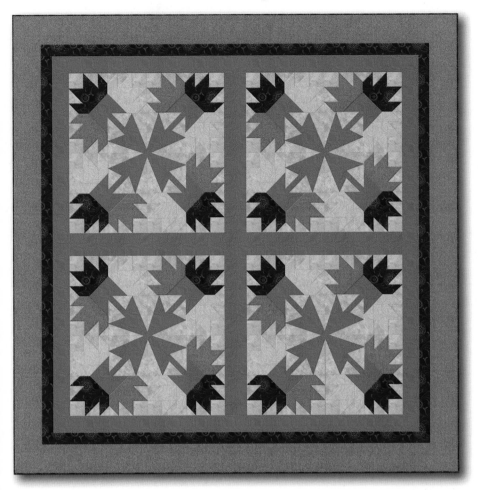

Approximate Size:
45 ½" x 45 ½"

Technique:
Foundation Piecing

Blocks:
Lily Bouquet (page 16)

Block Size:
8" x 8"

MATERIALS:
1 yard purple
1 ½ yards pink
½ yard yellow
1 yard light green
1 yard medium green
2 ¼ yards backing
Batting

CUTTING:
Blocks
Note: *You don't need to cut exact pieces for foundation piecing.*

Finishing
2 strips, 2" x 16 ½", medium green (sashing)
3 strips, 2" x 34", medium green (sashing/border)
2 strips, 2" x 37 ½", medium green (sashing/border)
4 strips, 2"-wide, purple (first border)
4 strips, 3 ½"-wide, pink (second border)
4 strips, 2 ½"-wide, pink (binding)

INSTRUCTIONS:
1. Referring to Foundation Piecing on the CD, make 16 Lily Bouquet blocks.

2. Referring to photo, sew four blocks together; repeat three more times.

3. Sew blocks together with a 2" x 16 ½" green sashing strip in between. Repeat.

4. Sew rows together with a 2" x 16 ½" green sashing strip in between. Sew remaining green strips to sides of quilt; sew 2" x 37 ½" green strips to top and bottom.

5. Sew remaining borders to quilt top sides first, then top and bottom.

6. Finish quilt referring to Finishing your Quilt on the CD.

Elegance

Picture Appliqué

Approximate Size:
32 ½" x 32 ½"

Technique:
Picture Appliqué

Blocks:
Regal Rose (page 25)

Pretty Flower (page 24)

Rose Bud (page 28)

5-Petal Flower (page 25)

Block Size:
10" x 10"

MATERIALS:
⅝ yard light blue (background)

½ yard red

⅜ yard burgundy

fat quarters yellow, light pink, medium pink, dark pink, orange

scraps of various shades of green

⅜ yard dark green (sashing/first border)

1 yard backing

Batting

CUTTING:
Blocks

4 squares, 10 ½" x 10 ½", light blue (background squares)

Finishing

2 strips, 2 ½" x 10 ½", dark green (sashing)

3 strips, 2 ½" x 22 ½", dark green (sashing)

2 strips, 2 ½" x 26 ½", dark green (sashing)

4 strips, 3 ½"-wide, red (border)

4 strips, 2 ½"-wide, burgundy (binding)

INSTRUCTIONS:

1. Prepare appliqué pieces according to your favorite Appliqué method on the enclosed CD. Appliqué pieces to background squares.

2. Referring to photo, sew two blocks together with a 2 ½" x 10" dark green sashing strip in between. Repeat.

3. Sew the rows of blocks together with a 2 ½" x 22 ½" dark green sashing strip in between. Sew the remaining 2 ½" x 26 ½" dark green sashing strips to the sides of the quilt top.

4. Sew the red border strips to quilt top sides first, then top and bottom.

5. Finish quilt referring to Finishing your Quilt on the CD.

Flower Garden
Traditional Appliqué

Approximate Size:
44 ½" x 55 ½"

Technique:
Traditional Appliqué

Blocks:
Whig Rose (page 32)
Hibiscus (page 29)
Victorian Rose (page 31)

Block Size:
8" x 8"

MATERIALS:
½ yard white (background)
1 ½ yards cream (background)
½ yard dk green (background)
fat quarter light green, yellow
3 yards pink
½ yard red
scraps gold and orange
Batting

CUTTING:
Blocks
4 squares, 8 ½" x 8 ½", white (background)
8 squares, 8 ½" x 8 ½", cream (Background)
5 squares, 8 ½" x 8 ½", dk green (Background)

Finishing
2 squares, 13" x 13", pink (cut in quarters diagonally)
2 squares, 13 ½" x 13 ½", pink (cut in half diagonally)
8 strips, 2 ½"-wide, dark green (first border)
8 strips, 3 ½"-wide, cream (second border)
8 strips, 2 ½"-wide, pink (binding)

INSTRUCTIONS:
1. Prepare all applique pieces according to your favorite Appliqué method on the enclosed CD. Appliqué pieces to background squares.

2. Referring to photo, arrange blocks in diagonal rows with smaller pink triangles at ends (they will be oversized and need to be trimmed). Sew rows together. Sew large triangles at each corner; trim triangles even with sides.

3. Sew first border to quilt top sides first, then top and bottom. Repeat for second border.

4. Finish quilt referring to Finishing your Quilt on the CD.

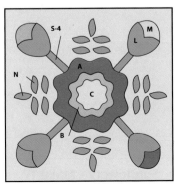

Make 8 Whig Rose

Make 4 Hibiscus

Make 5 Victorian Rose

Sunny Fields
Patchwork

Approximate Size:
75 ½" x 99 ½"

Technique:
Patchwork

Blocks:
Sunflowers (page 47)
Winter Rose Poinsettia (page 52)

Block Size:
12" x 12"

MATERIALS:
½ yard yellow
2 ½ yards gold
2 yards orange
3 yards lt purple
1 ¼ yards dk purple
3 yards green
¾ yard backing
Batting

INSTRUCTIONS:
1. Make 18 Winter Rose Poinsettia blocks and 17 Sunflowers blocks using the 12" templates on the CD.

2. Referring to photo, sew blocks together in rows, then sew rows together.

3. Sew borders to quilt top sides first, then top and bottom.

4. Finish quilt referring to Finishing your Quilt on the CD.

CUTTING:
Blocks

Sunflowers
17 C Squares, gold
68 E Squares, gold
68 F Rectangles, gold
272 G Triangles, gold
272 D Triangles, orange
272 G Triangles, orange
136 G Triangles, yellow

Winter Rose Poinsettia
18 C Squares, gold
72 G Triangles, orange
216 D Triangles, lt purple
288 D Triangles, dk purple
72 F Rectangles, dk purple
72 C Squares, green
72 D Triangles, green
144 E Squares, green
144 G Triangles, green

Finishing
8 strips, 2"-wide, dk purple (first border)
8 strips, 2 ½"-wide, green (second border)
10 strips, 4 ½"-wide, lt purple (third border)
10 strips, 2 ½"-wide, lt purple (binding)

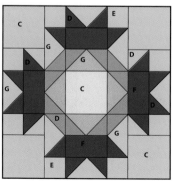

Winter Rose Poinsettia - Make 18

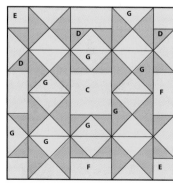

Sunflowers - Make 17

Windblown Flowers
Foundation Piecing and Patchwork

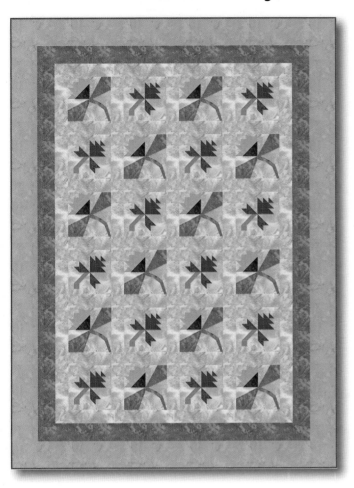

Approximate Size:
56 ½" x 25 ½"

Techniques:
Foundation Piecing and Patchwork

Blocks:
Blooming Flower (page 20)
Windblown Lily (page 52)

Block Size:
8" x 8"

MATERIALS:
3 yards light blue
1 yard red
2 yards pink
½ yard lt green

1 ¾ yards med green
¼ yard purple
¾ yard backing
Batting

INSTRUCTIONS:
1. Make 12 Blooming Flower blocks referring to Foundation Piecing and using the 8" foundation pattern on the CD. Make 12 Windblown Lilly blocks using the 8" templates on the CD.

2. Referring to photo, sew blocks together with 2 ½" x 8 ½" lt blue sashing strips in between.

3. Sew the rows of blocks together with 2 ½" x 42 ½" lt blue strips in between.

4. Sew the 2 ½"-wide lt blue border strips to the sides and then to the top and bottom of the quilt.

5. Sew the med green and pink borders to quilt top sides first, then top and bottom.

6. Finish quilt referring to Finishing your Quilt on the CD.

CUTTING:
Blocks

Windblown Lily
60 D Triangles, red
48 E Squares, red
48 D Triangles, lt green
12 E Square, lt green
24 B Triangles, med green
24 D Triangles, med green
48 B Triangles, lt blue
48 C Squares, lt blue
108 D triangles, lt blue
84 E Squares, lt blue
84 F Rectangles, lt blue

Blooming Flower
Note: *You do not need to cut exact pieces for foundation piecing.*

Finishing
18 strips, 2 ½" x 8 ½", lt blue (sashing)
5 strips, 2 ½" x 42 ½", lt blue (sashing)
6 strips, 2 ½" -wide lt blue (first border)
8 strips, 3 ½"-wide med green (second border)
9 strips, 4 ½"-wide, pink (third border)
9 strips, 2 ½"-wide, red (binding)

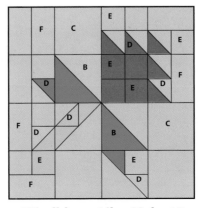

Windblown Lily - Make 12

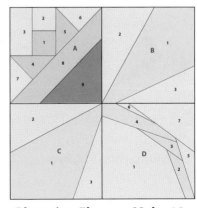

Blooming Flower - Make 12

Floral Placemats

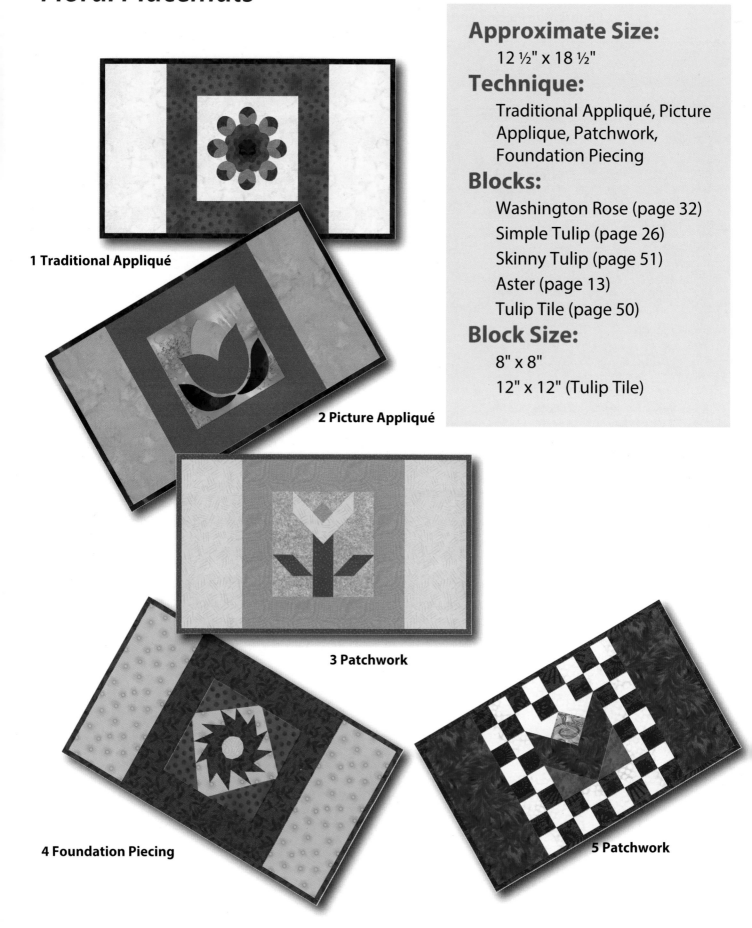

1 Traditional Appliqué

2 Picture Appliqué

3 Patchwork

4 Foundation Piecing

5 Patchwork

Approximate Size:
  12 ½" x 18 ½"

Technique:
  Traditional Appliqué, Picture Applique, Patchwork, Foundation Piecing

Blocks:
  Washington Rose (page 32)
  Simple Tulip (page 26)
  Skinny Tulip (page 51)
  Aster (page 13)
  Tulip Tile (page 50)

Block Size:
  8" x 8"
  12" x 12" (Tulip Tile)

MATERIALS:

Fat quarters of each fabric needed for your block

*¼ yard coordinating fabric 1 (block border)

⅛ yard coordinating fabric 2 (side border)

¼ yard contrasting fabric (binding)

½ yard backing

Batting

*Placemat 5 does not use this fabric.

CUTTING:

Blocks

Washington Rose (8" x 8" finished)

1 square, 8 ½" x 8 ½", cream

Simple Tulip (8" x 8" finished)

1 square, 8 ½" x 8 ½", aqua

Skinny Tulip (8" x 8" finished)

2 G Triangles, orange

4 B Triangles, yellow

4 G Triangles, yellow

4 B Triangles, green

2 C Squares, green

3 G Triangles, green

8 B Triangles, blue

12 C Squares, blue

3 G Triangles, blue

Aster (8" x 8" finished)

Note: *You do not need to cut exact pieces for foundation piecing.*

Tulip Tile (12" x 12" finished)

4 D Triangles, pink

4 B Triangles, red

2 B Triangles, green

4 D Triangles, white

24 E Squares, white

24 E Squares, purple

Finishing

*2 strips, 2 ½" x 8 ½", coordinating fabric 1

*2 strips, 2 ½" x 12 ½", coordinating fabric 1

2 strips, 3 ½" x 12 ½", coordinating fabric 2

1 rectangle, 12 ½" x 18 ½" backing

2 strips, 2 ½"-wide, contrasting fabric (binding)

*Omit these strips for Placemat 5, Tulip Tile.

INSTRUCTIONS:

1. Make quilt block referring to instructions and using patterns on the CD.

2. For Placemats 1 to 4, sew 2 ½" x 8 ½" strips to sides of block. Sew 2 ½" x 12 ½" strips to top and bottom of block.

For Placemat 5, sew 3 ½" x 12 ½" strips to sides (not top and bottom) of block.

3. Sew 3 ½" x 12 ½" strips to sides of block to finish placemat top.

4. Finish placemats referring to Finishing your Quilt on the CD.

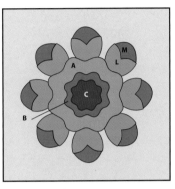

Washington Rose

Simple Tulip

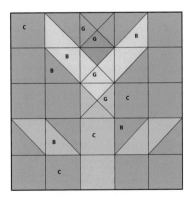

Skinny Tulip

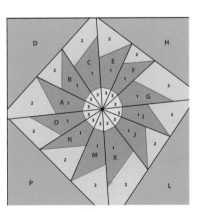

Aster

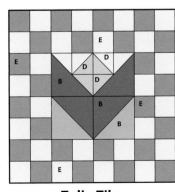

Tulip Tile

Index

About the CD

To run this application on Windows:

This is a self-loading CD. Simply place the CD into the CD-ROM drive. If the Auto-Run feature is not active on your system, follow these instructions to install:

• Click the Start button.

• Select Run from the menu.

• When the Run window opens, click Browse.

• Select your CD-ROM drive and then select 100 Flower Blocks..

• Click OK and follow the onscreen instructions.

• Decide which Blocks you are making and choose the template patterns that you need to complete it, double click to open.

• If the block does not open, you may need to install Acrobat Reader. Download it easily from the internet using the website: http://www.adobe.com/products/acrobat/readstep2.html

• Print the template patterns you will need for your project.

To run this application on Mac OS 9 and OS X:

• Insert the CD into the CD-ROM drive. Double click on the *100 Flower Blocks* icon when it appears on the desktop.

• Choose the folder name that corresponds to the section that your block is in and click to open.

• Look for the Template folder and choose the templates that you need to make your blocks.

• If the block does not open, you may need to install Acrobat Reader. Download it easily from the internet using the website: http://www.adobe.com/products/acrobat/readstep2.html

• Print the number of blocks and patterns you will need for your project.

For additional information and instructions, please read Frequently Asked Questions (FAQ.pdf) on the CD.